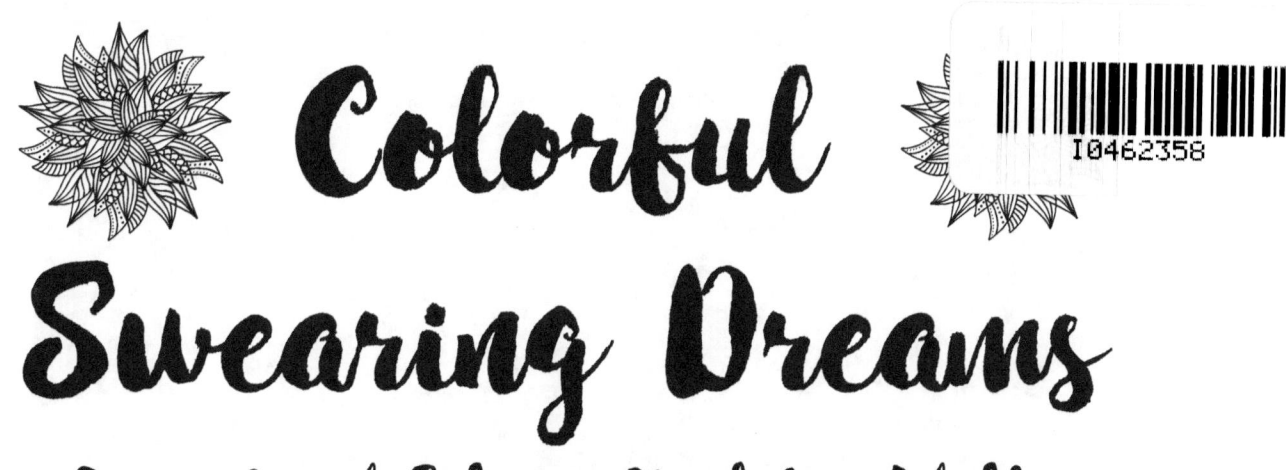

Colorful Swearing Dreams

Swear Word Coloring Book for Adults

IS YOUR STRESS LEVEL HIGH?
DO YOU WANT TO SWEAR OUT LOUD
TO LEVEL IT DOWN?
THIS BOOK WILL KICK YOUR STRESS AWAY!

Multiple studies revealed that coloring mandalas, geometric patterns & other shapes helps reduce stress and anxiety for adults.

This swear word coloring book will allow you to enter in a relaxed state by focusing in what you are doing and blocking out the nonstop thinking or other distractions. Those swear word designs will make you laugh and relieve your stress by expelling your negative thoughts.

This book contains 20 pages of beautiful & intricate designs mixing up with funny swear words that will connect with you.
Each page is single-sided for getting the best coloring experience.

TIME TO COLOR THE STRESS AWAY!

Colorful
Swearing Dreams

Swear Word Coloring Book for Adults

Coloring Test Page

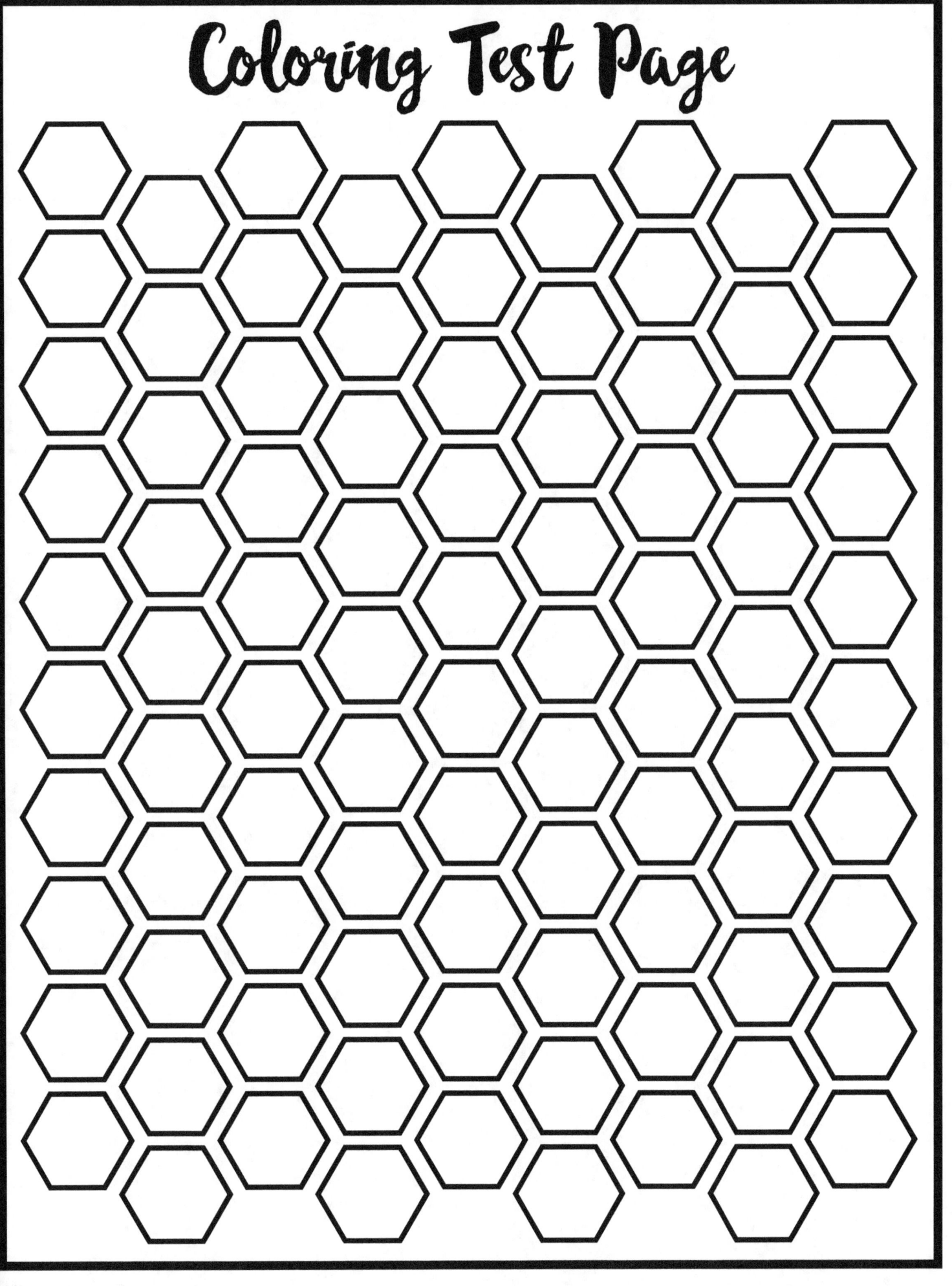

Colorful Swearing Dreams

Swear Word Coloring Book for Adults

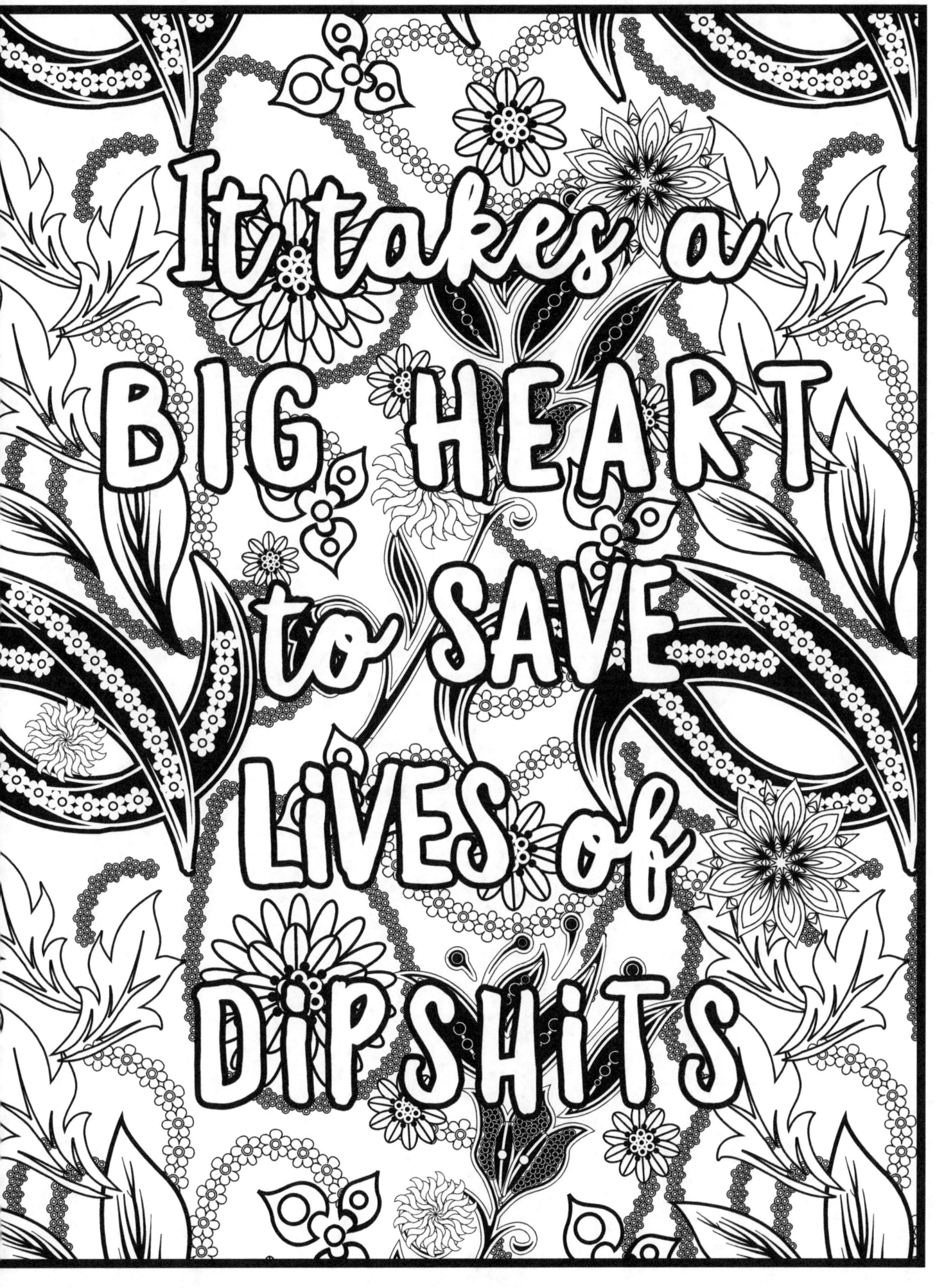

Colorful
Swearing Dreams

Swear Word Coloring Book for Adults

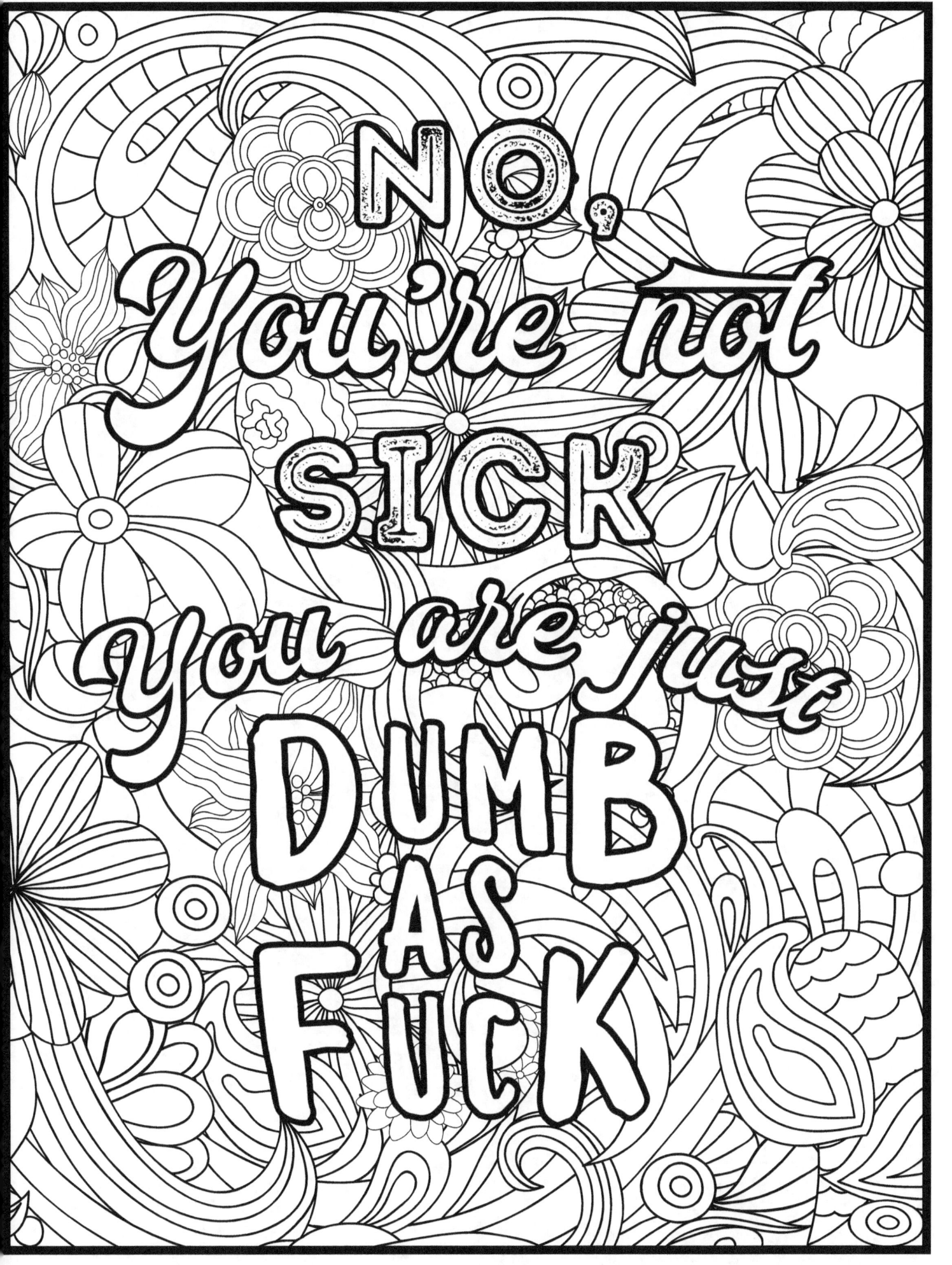

Colorful Swearing Dreams

Swear Word Coloring Book for Adults

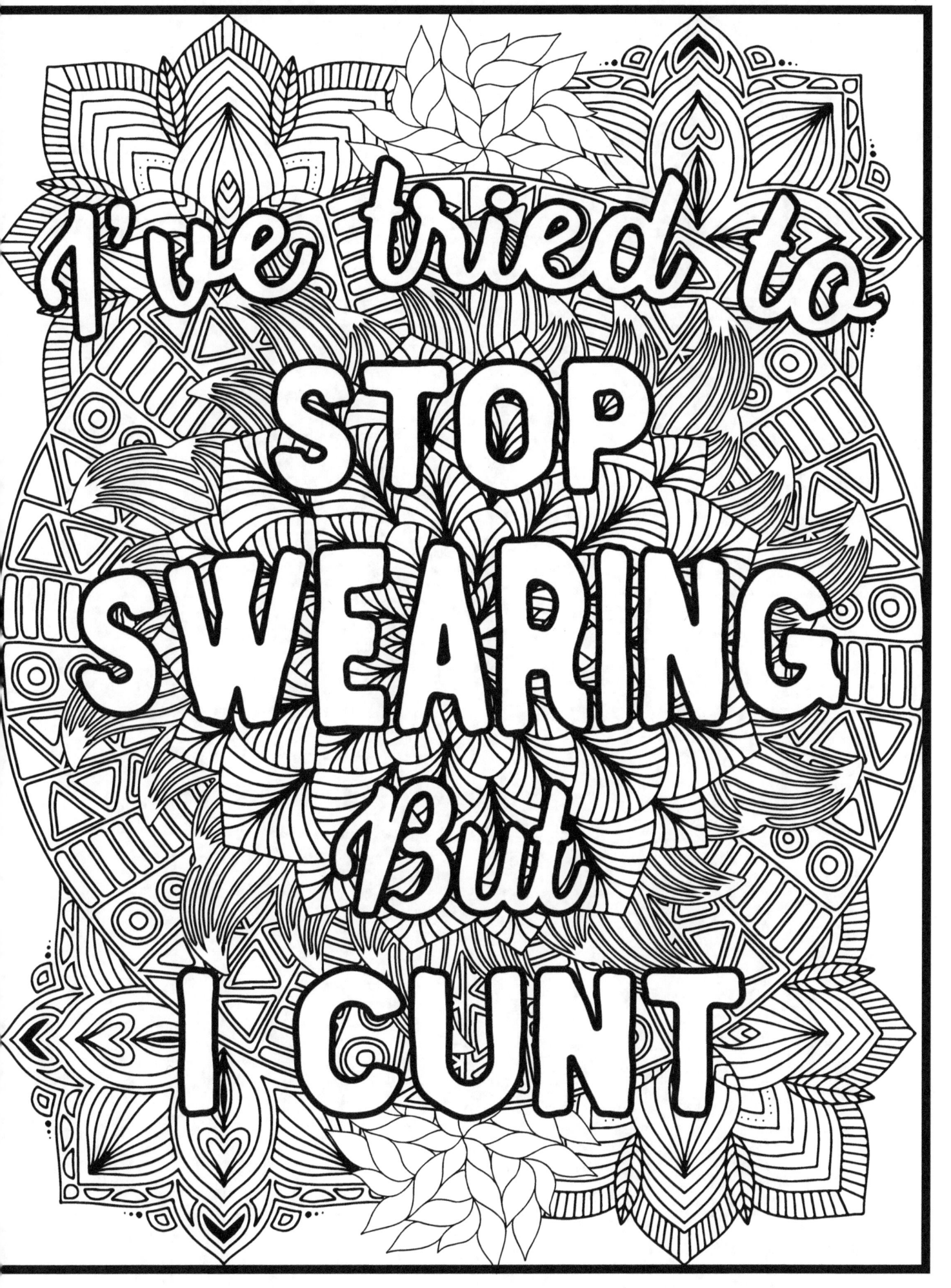

Colorful Swearing Dreams

Swear Word Coloring Book for Adults

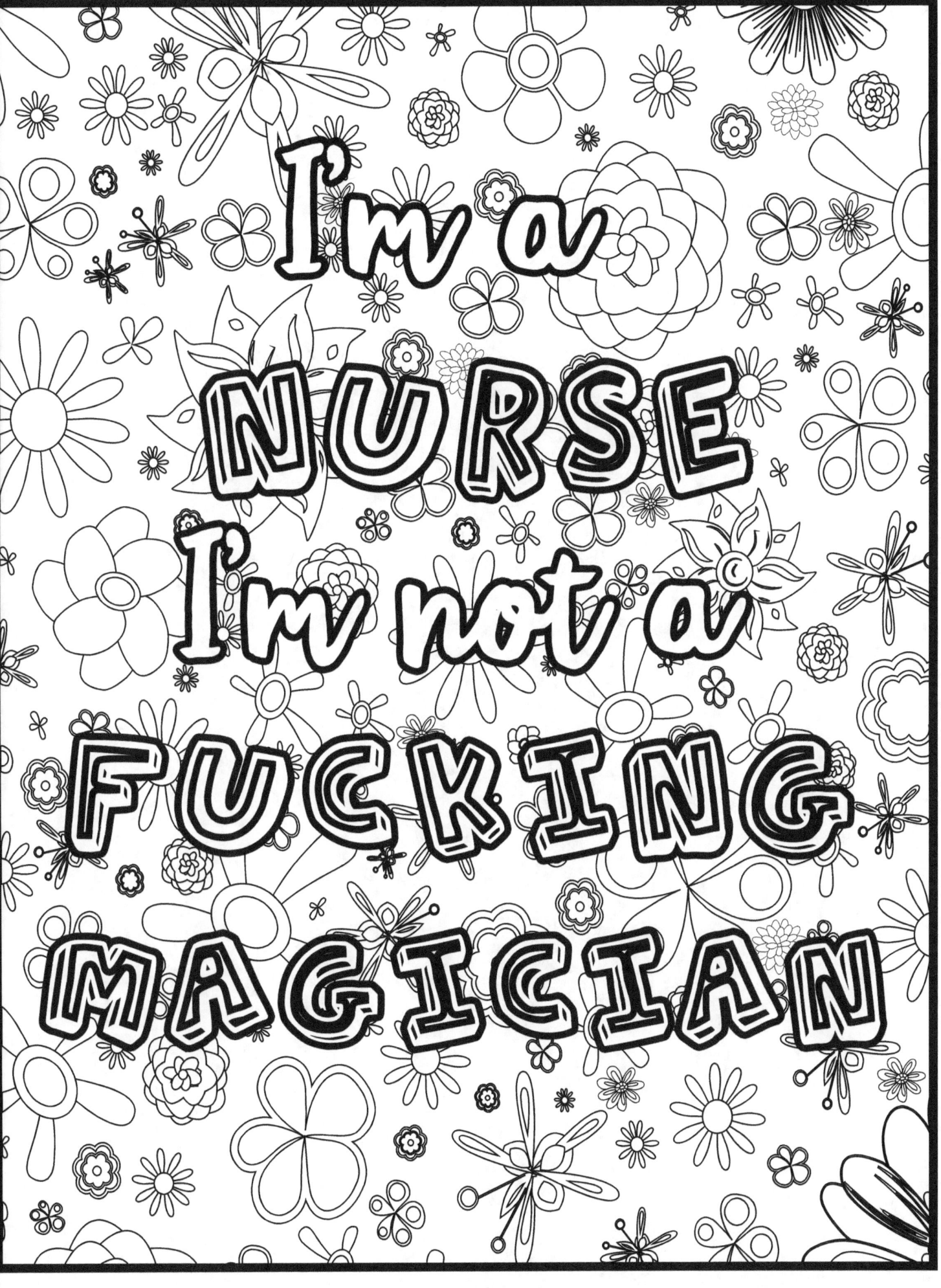

Colorful

Swearing Dreams

Swear Word Coloring Book for Adults

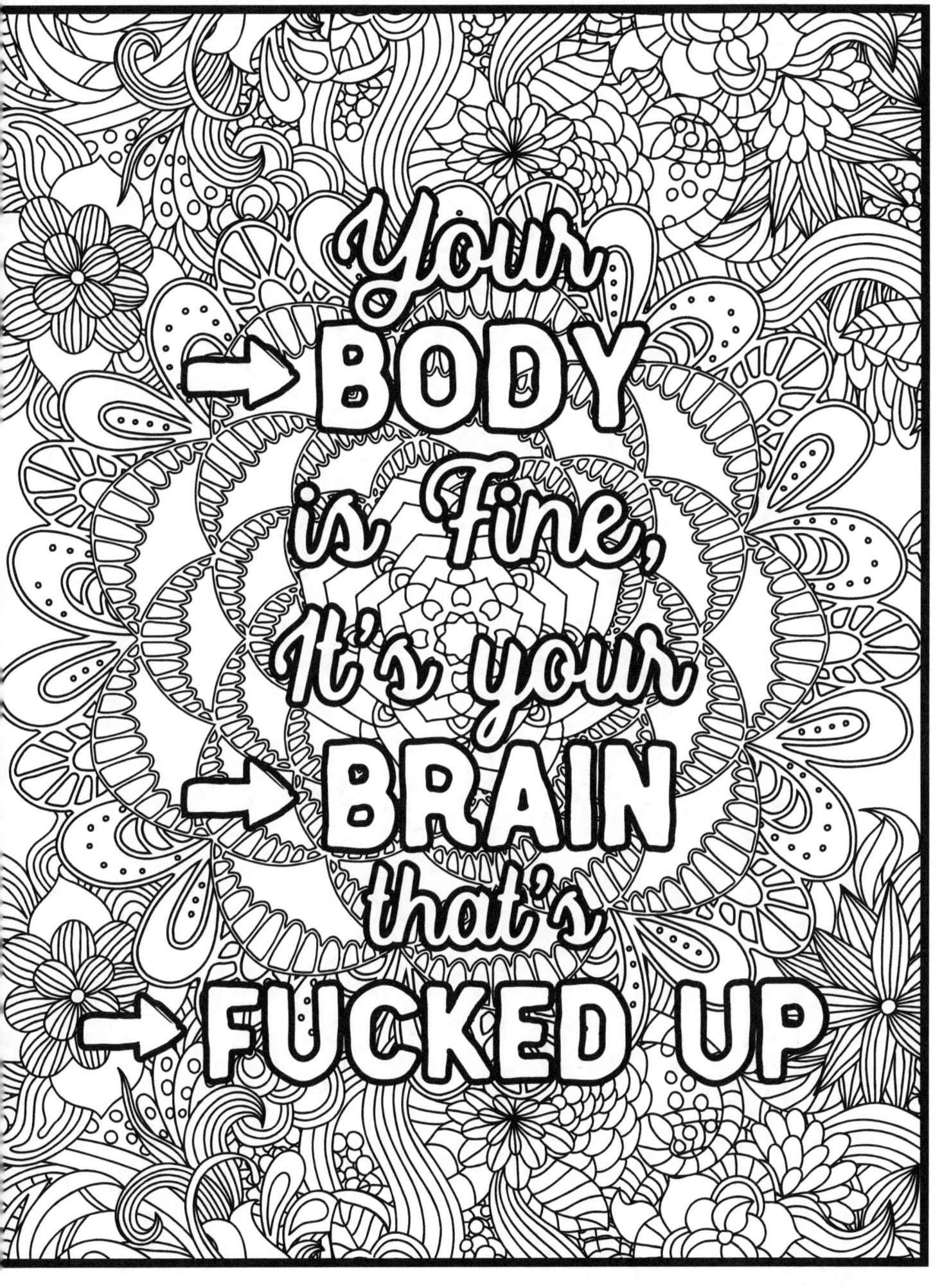

Colorful

Swearing Dreams

Swear Word Coloring Book for Adults

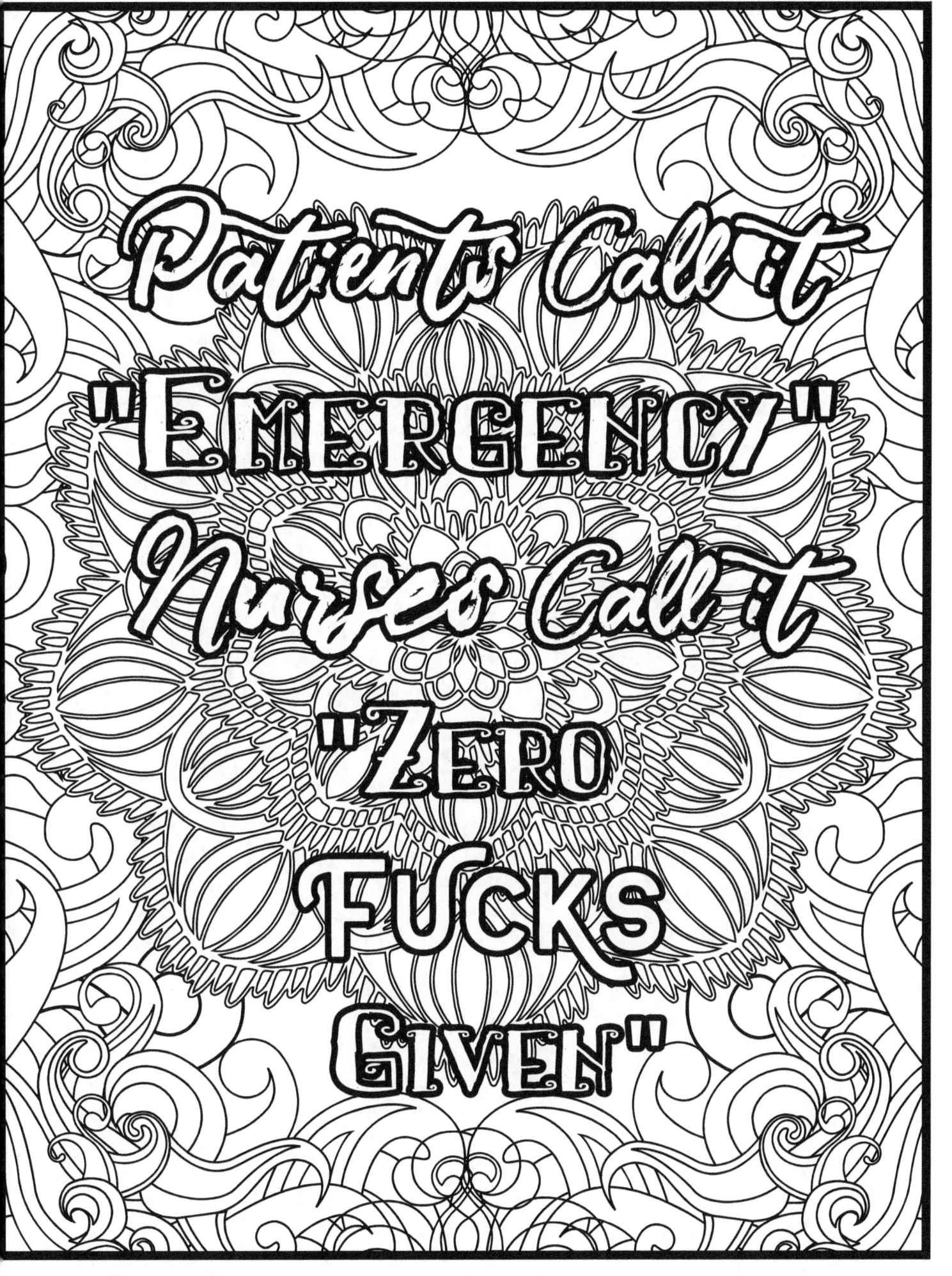

Colorful

Swearing Dreams

Swear Word Coloring Book for Adults

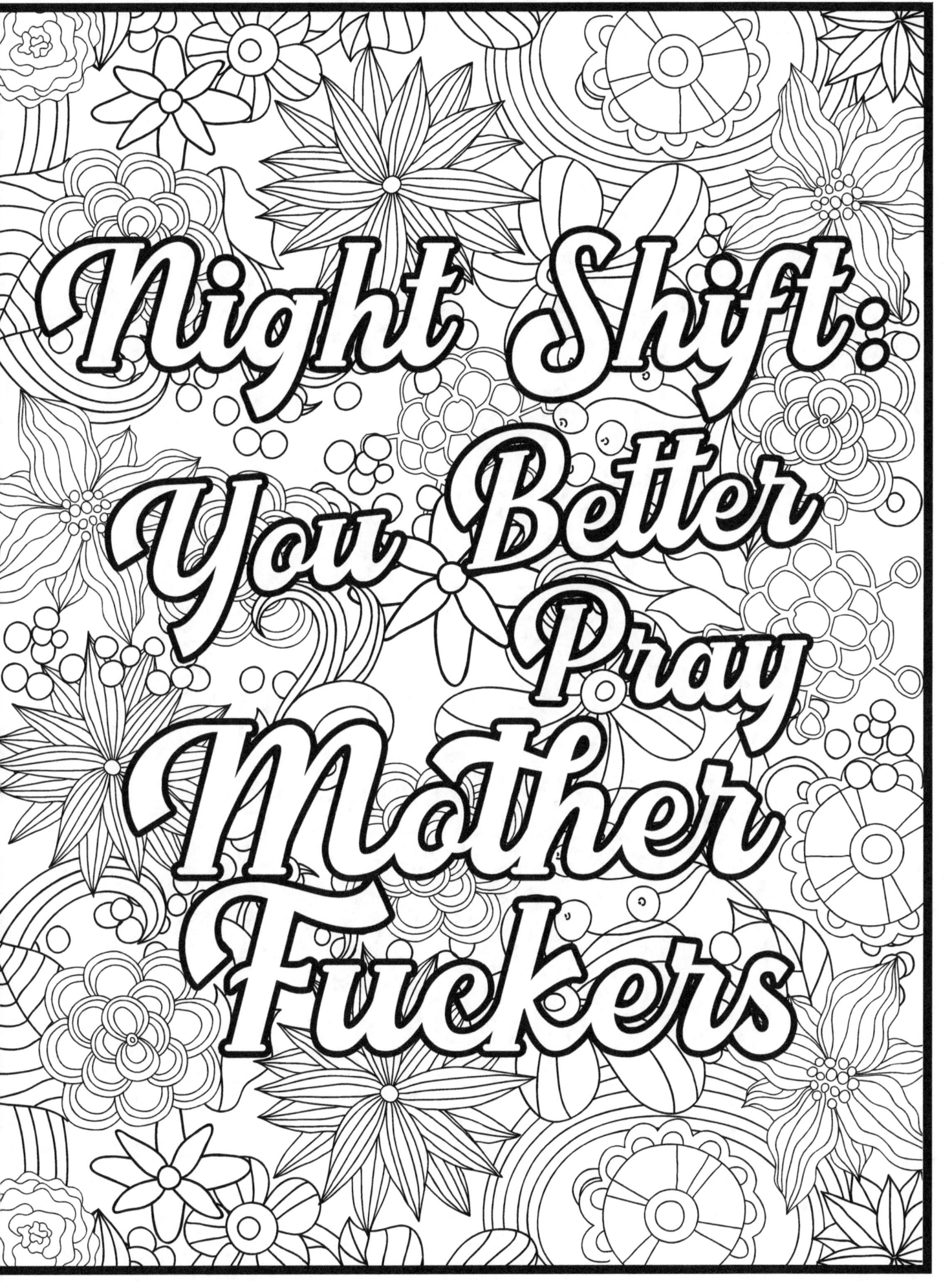

Colorful Swearing Dreams

Swear Word Coloring Book for Adults

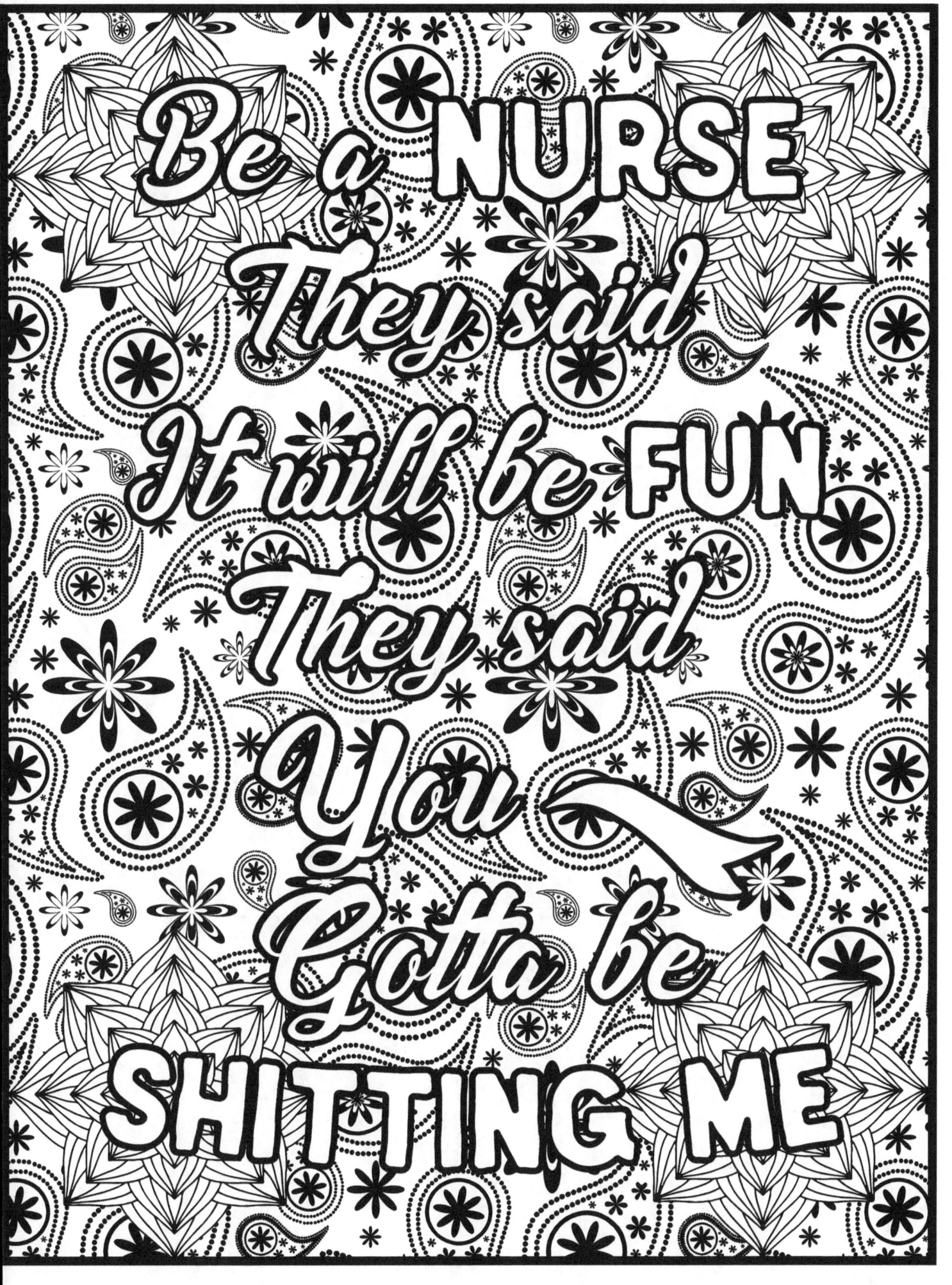

Colorful

Swearing Dreams

Swear Word Coloring Book for Adults

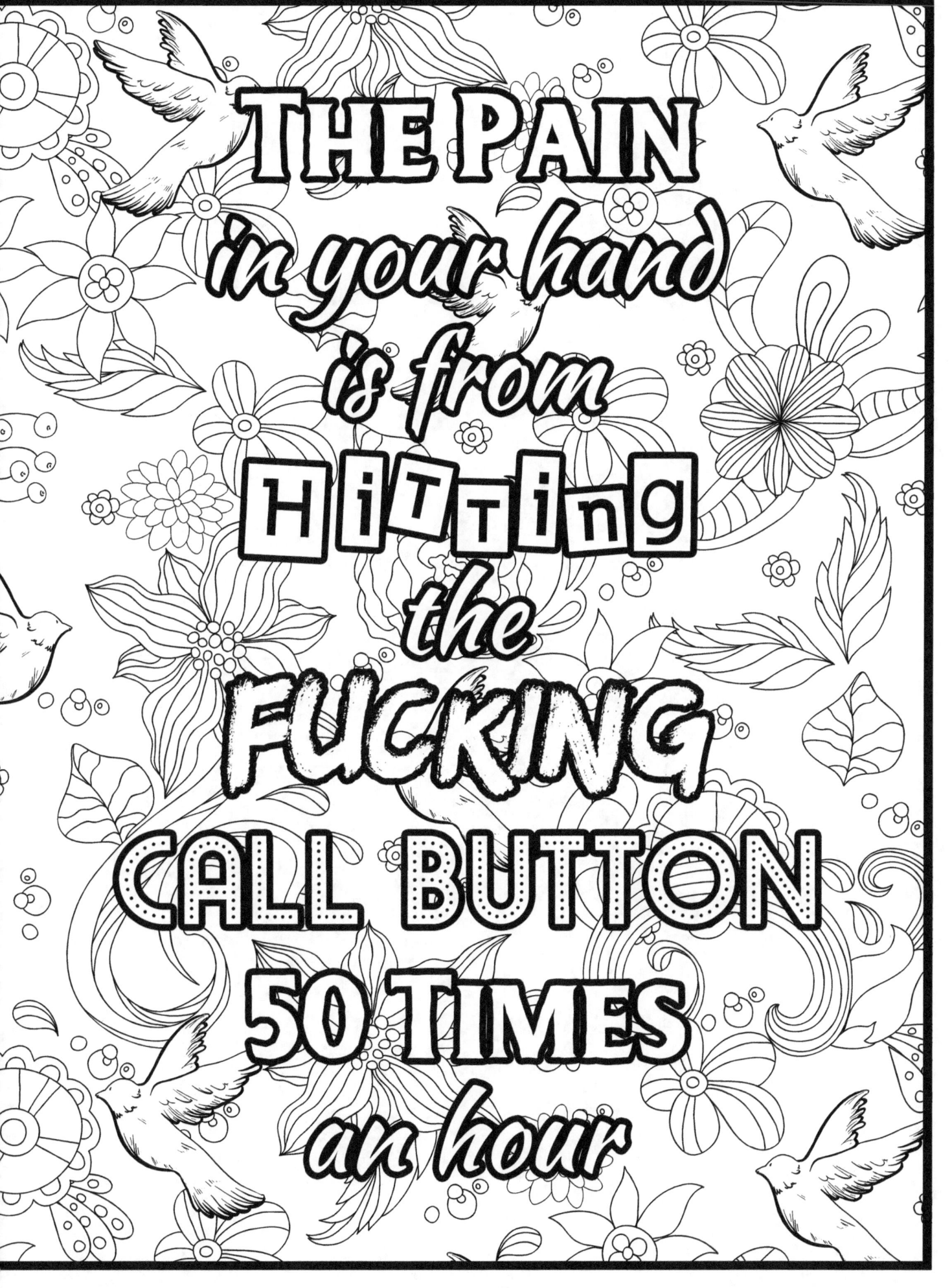

Colorful

Swearing Dreams

Swear Word Coloring Book for Adults

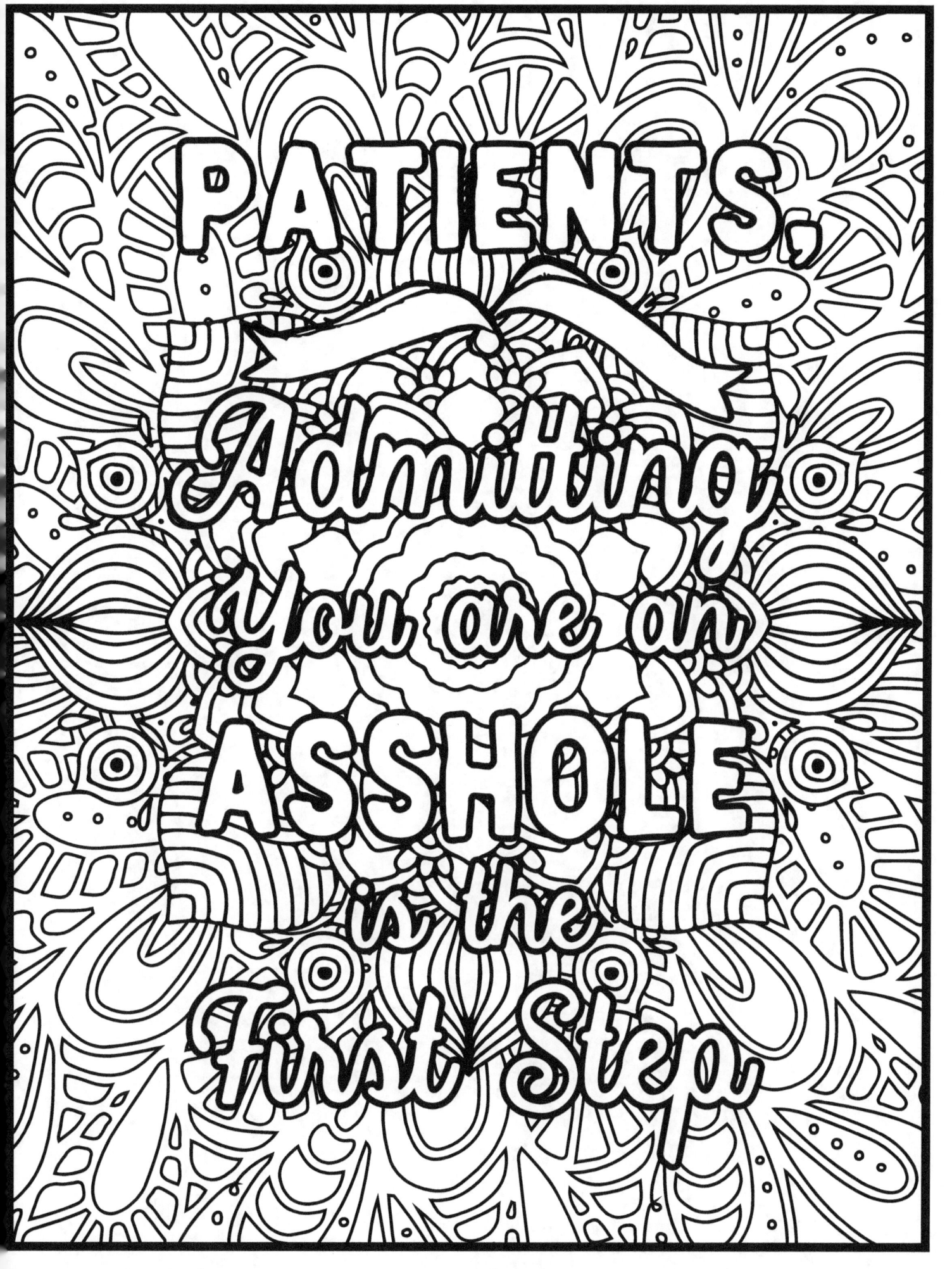

Colorful Swearing Dreams

Swear Word Coloring Book for Adults

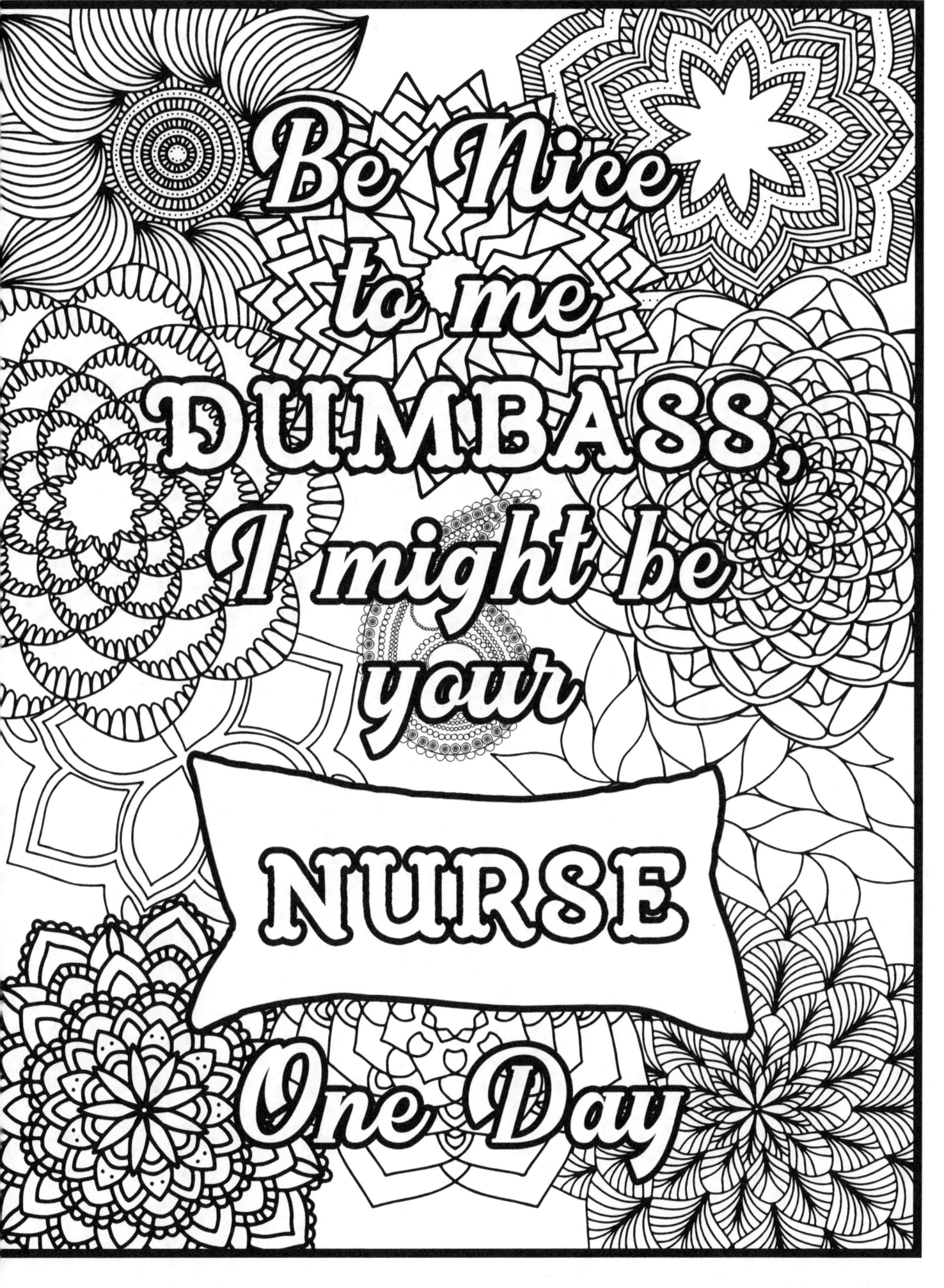

Colorful Swearing Dreams

Swear Word Coloring Book for Adults

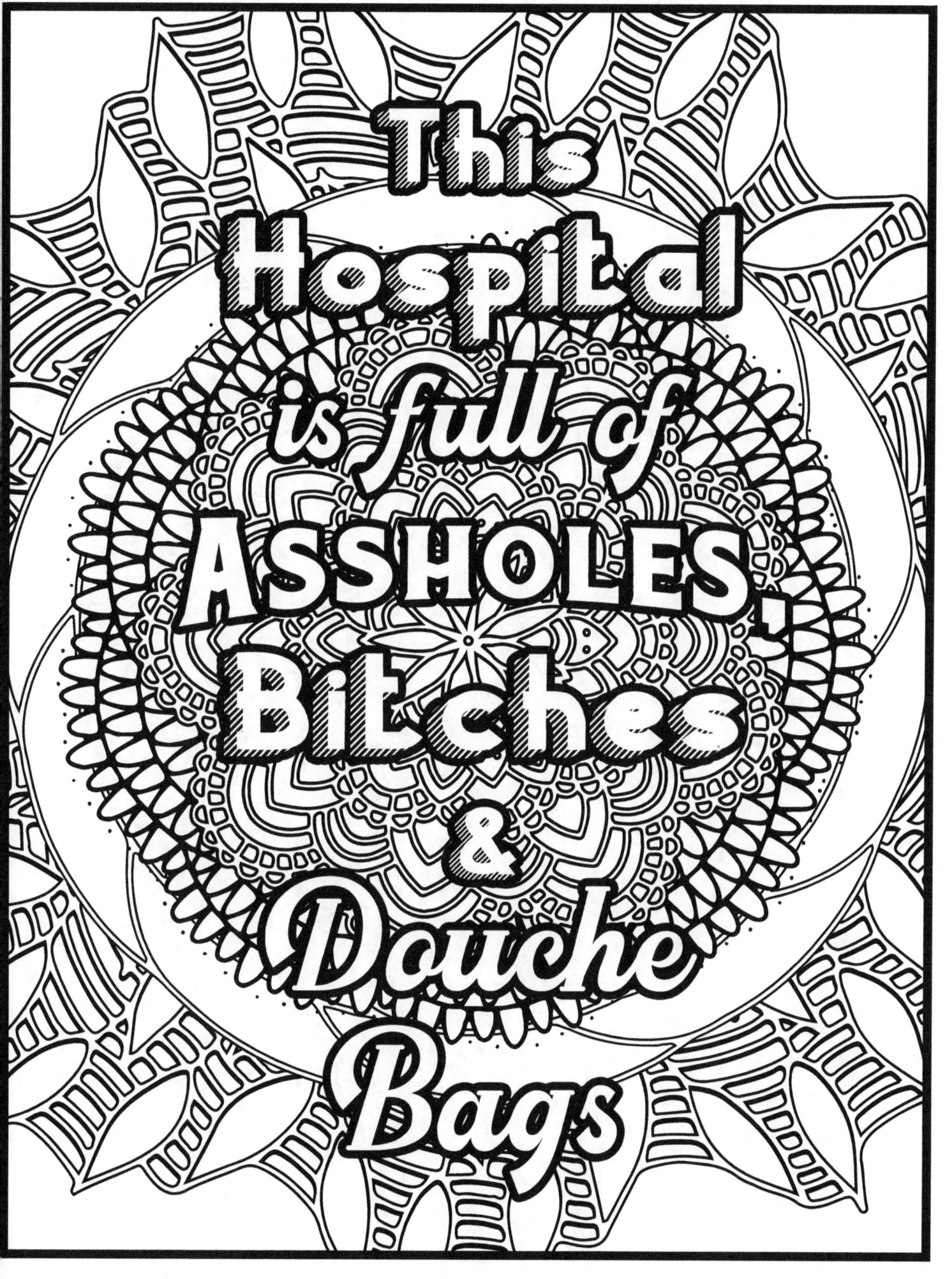

Colorful Swearing Dreams

Swear Word Coloring Book for Adults

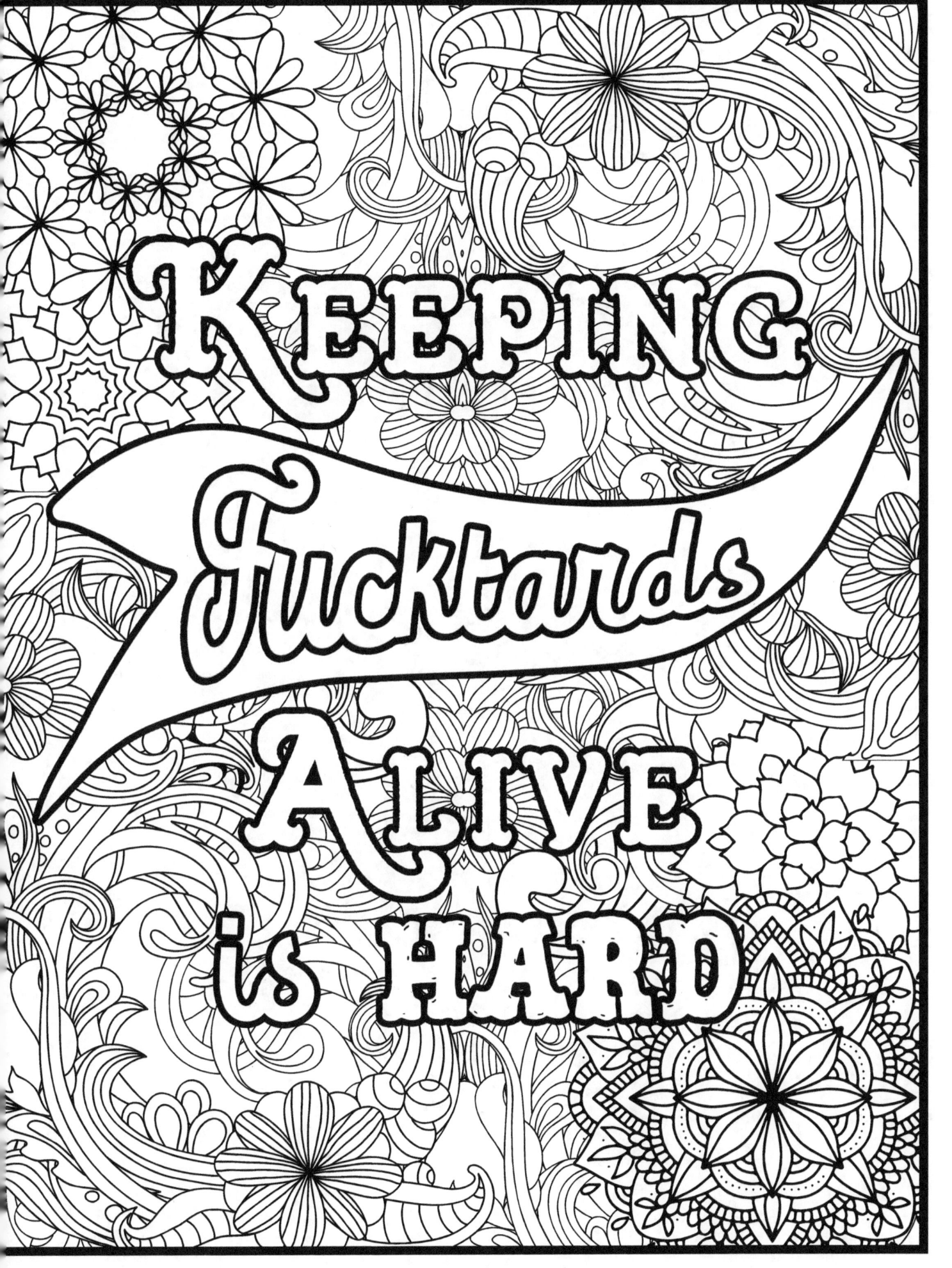

Colorful Swearing Dreams

Swear Word Coloring Book for Adults

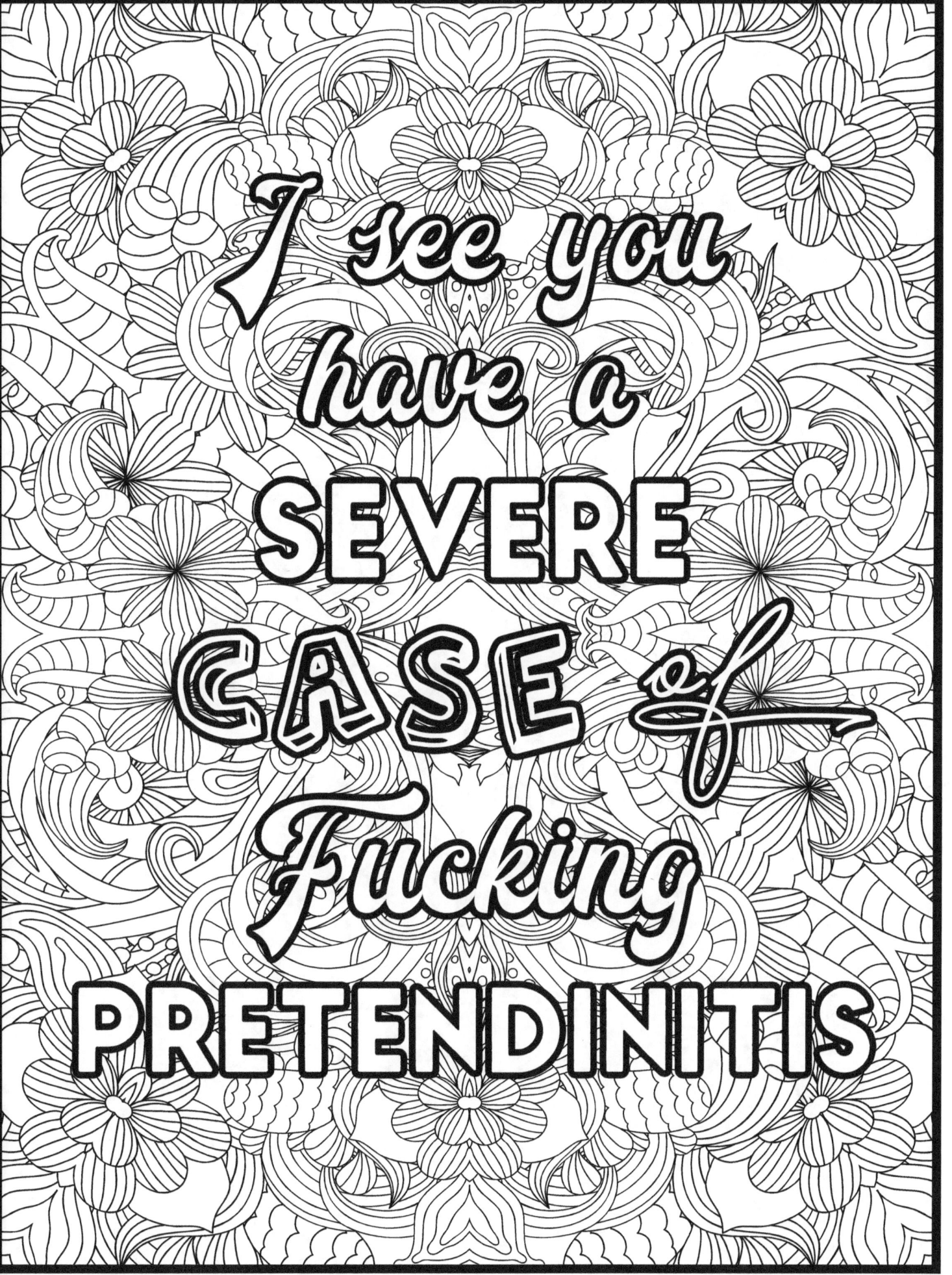

Colorful Swearing Dreams

Swear Word Coloring Book for Adults

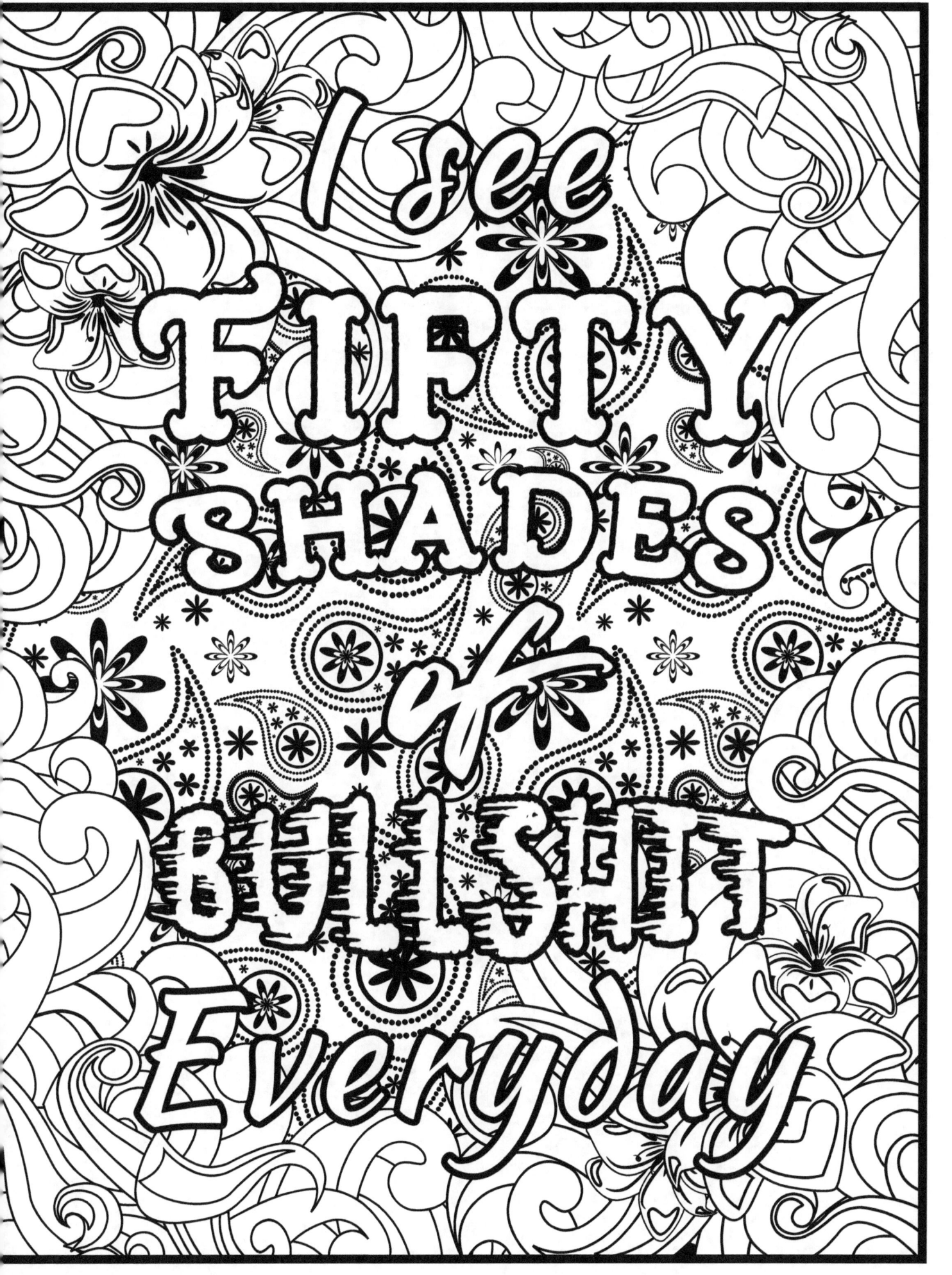

Colorful

Swearing Dreams

Swear Word Coloring Book for Adults

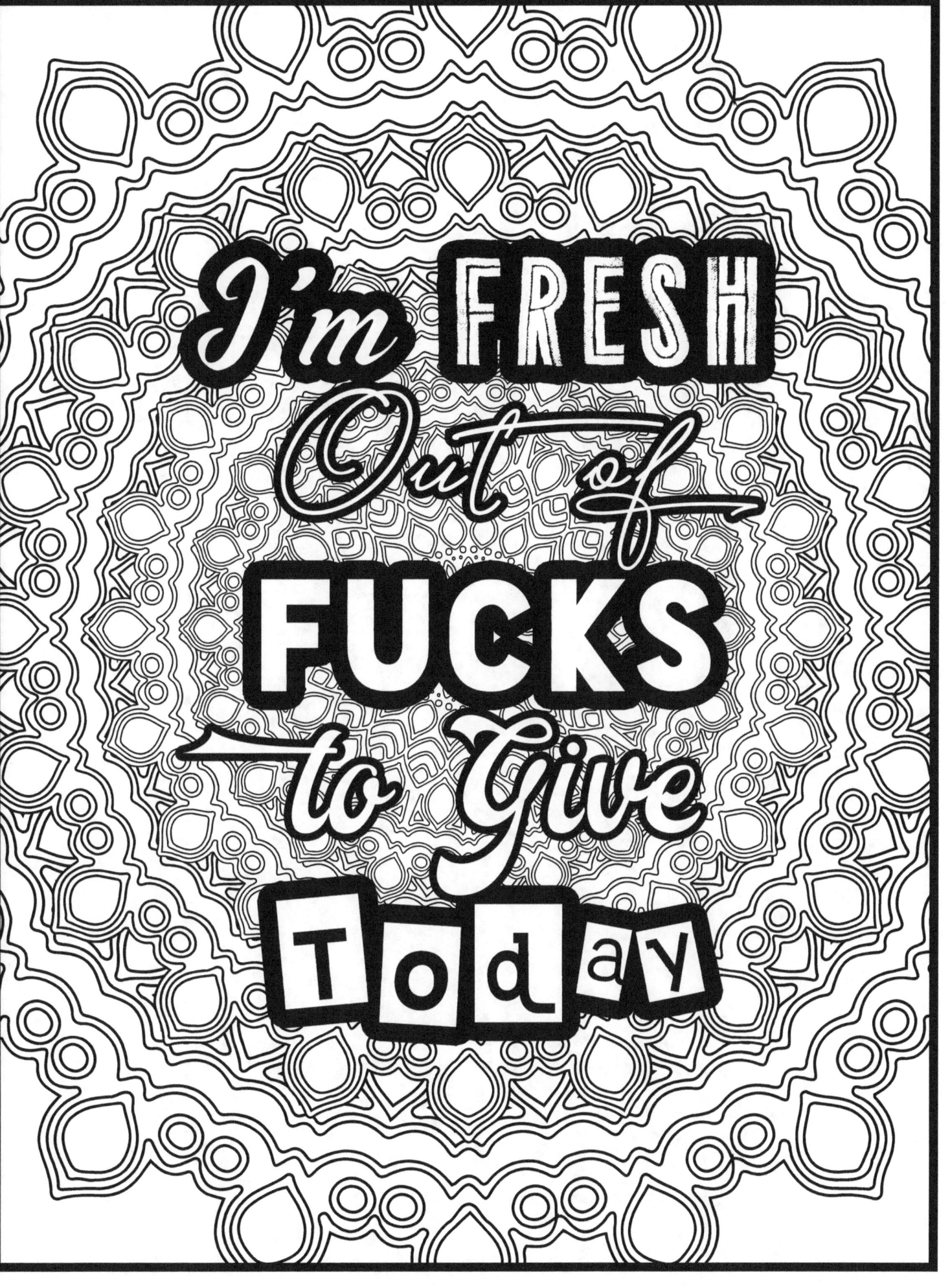

Colorful

Swearing Dreams

Swear Word Coloring Book for Adults

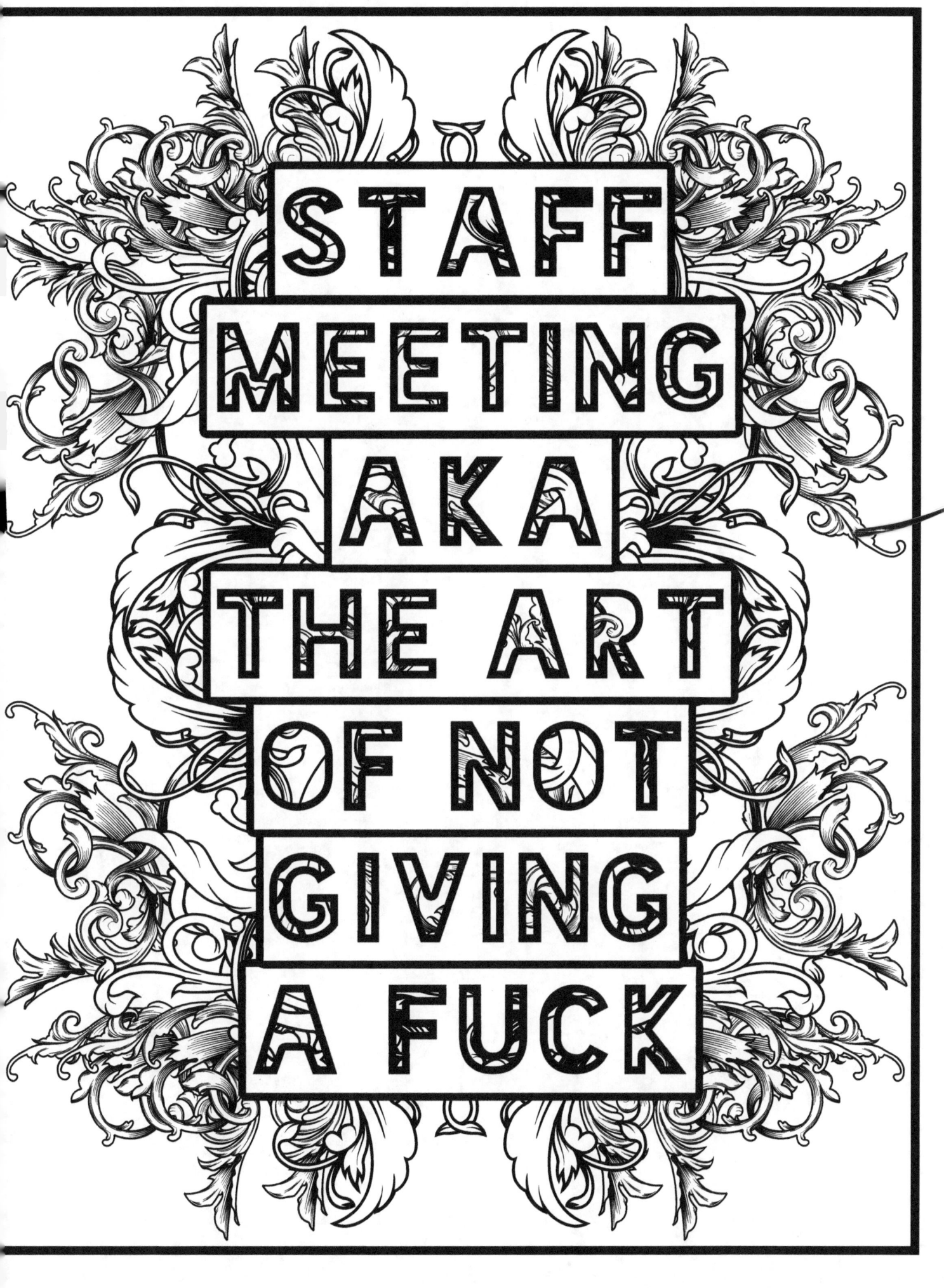

Colorful

Swearing Dreams

Swear Word Coloring Book for Adults

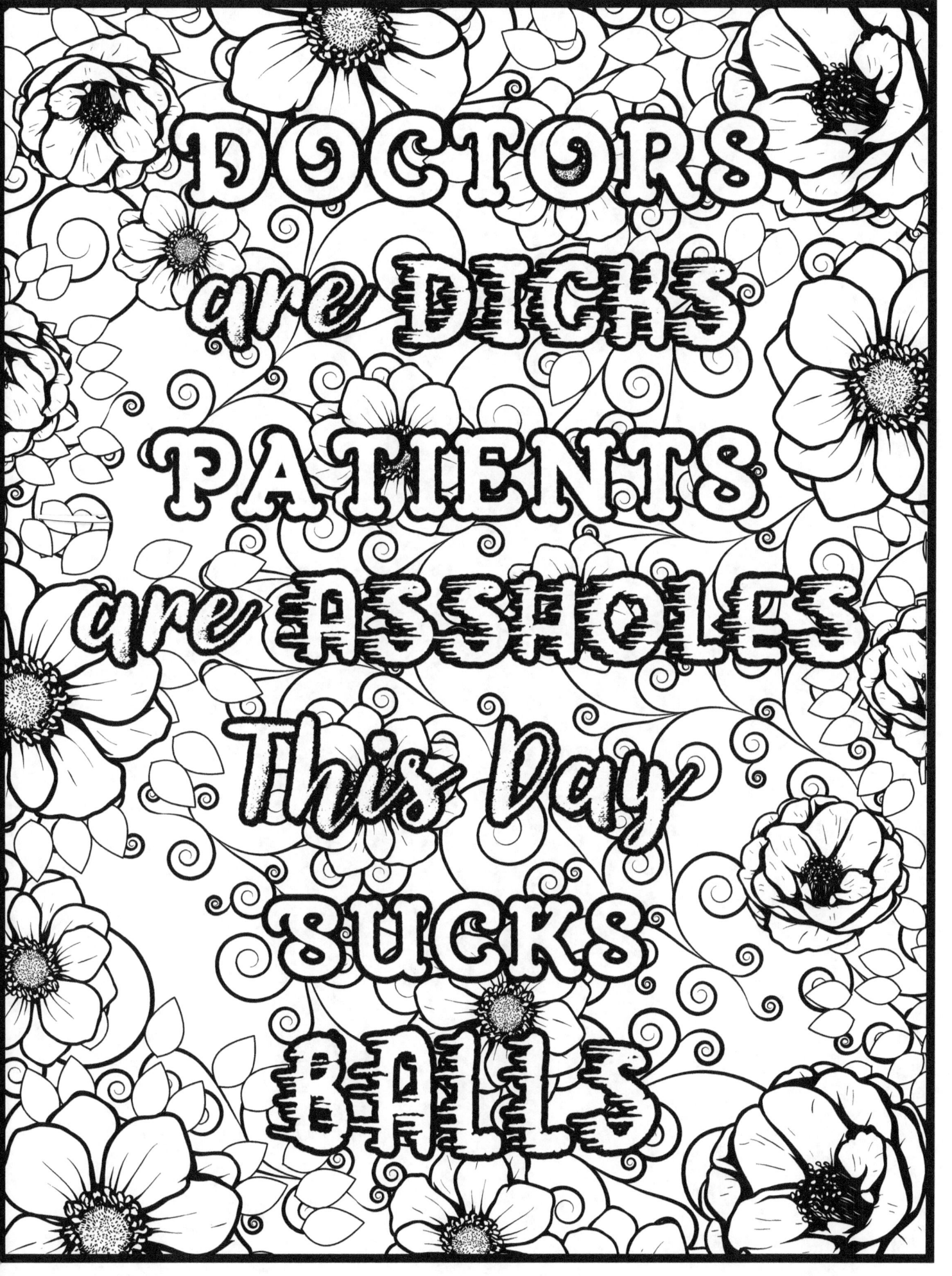

Colorful

Swearing Dreams

Swear Word Coloring Book for Adults

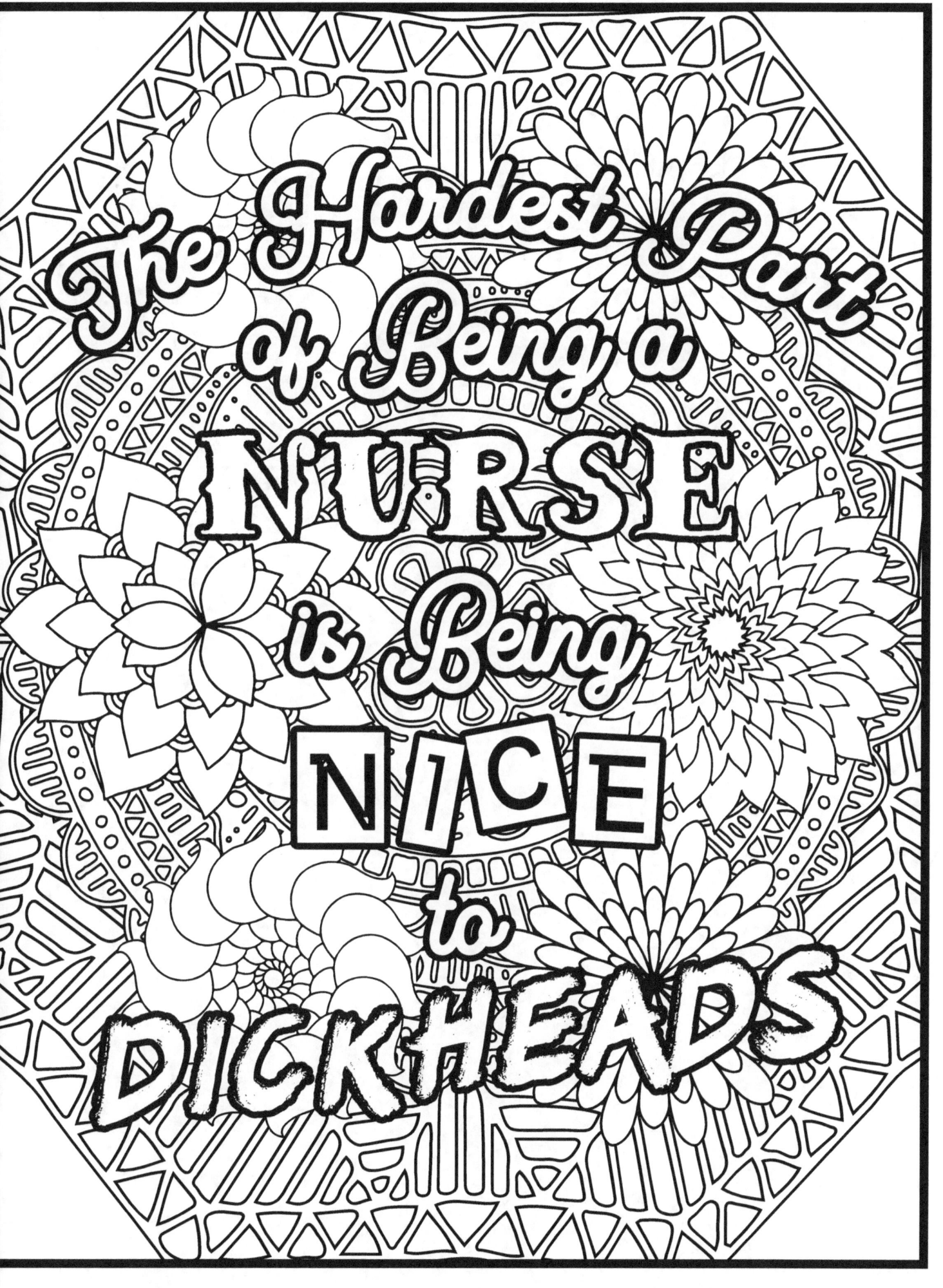

Colorful

Swearing Dreams

Swear Word Coloring Book for Adults

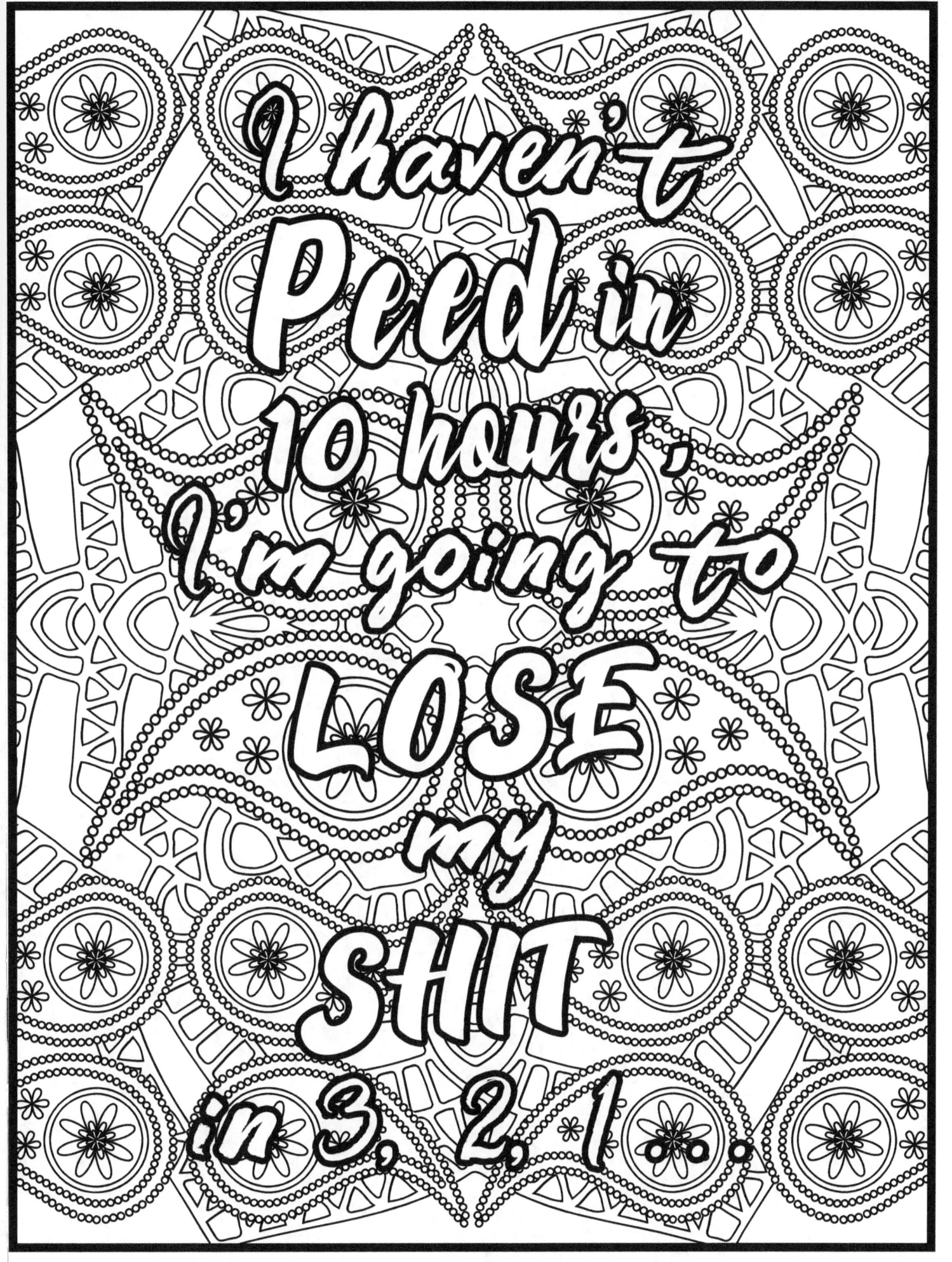

Colorful

Swearing Dreams

Swear Word Coloring Book for Adults